ASTRO-NUTS!

riddles about
astronauts and the
planets they love

written by
Rick Walton

illustrated by
Pat Bagley

Buckaroo Books
Carson City, Nevada

To Bob and Kristine Brown and their mission controllers Meagan, Jeremy, and Jacob, who are all having a blast way off in Florida.

©1995 Rick Walton
All rights reserved. No portion of this book
may be reproduced without written permission
from the publisher,
Buckaroo Books,
2533 North Carson Street, Suite 1544
Carson City, Nevada 89706.
Illustrations by Pat Bagley
Designed by Richard Erickson and Pat Bagley

Library of Congress Cataloging-in-Publication Data
Astro-nuts! : riddles about astronauts and the planets they love / by
Rick Walton
p.   cm.
1. Riddles, Juvenile. 2. Astronauts—Juvenile humor. 3. Outer
space—Juvenile humor. [1. Astronauts—Wit and humor. 2. Outer
space—Wit and humor. 3. Riddles. 4. Jokes.]   I. Title.
PN6371.5.W347
818'.5402--dc20   95-40680
                                         CIP   AC

5   4   3   2   1
Printed and bound in the United States
ISBN 1-882728-072

Q: How do astronauts communicate with Martians?

A: In Mars Code.

Q: How can you tell when the earth's afraid?

A: You can see its atmos-fear.

Q: What's very, very hot and has a hundred legs?

A: A sun-tipede.

Q: What's the scariest thing in space?

A: Mon-stars.

Q: What does the earth do when it sees a mon-star?

A: It quakes.

Q: What's the peskiest insect in the solar system?

A: The Marsquito.

Q: If you hate standing in lines, why should you go into space?

A: Because in space you'll be waitless.

Q: What do you get if you cross the sun with a rabbit's foot?

A: A lucky star.

Q: What planet comes in a can?

A: Nep-tuna.

Q: What should you eat Nep-tuna on?

A: Plu-toast.

Q: Which space travelers break easiest?

A: Glass-tronauts.

Q: What do astronauts like to eat for lunch?

A: Sunwiches.

Q: Where do astronauts eat their sunwiches?

A: At the lunchpad.

Q: Where do astronauts like to go fishing?

A: In the galax-sea.

Q: What do astronauts catch in the galax-sea?

A: Lob-stars, oy-stars, and starfish.

Q: What do astronauts use for bait?

A: Earthworms.

Q: Where do astronauts get their bait?

A: In wormholes.

Q: When the sun goes swimming, what does it do?

A: The sunstroke.

Q: What holds the moon in the sky?

A: Moonbeams.

Q: How does the solar system keep clean?

A: It takes meteor showers.

Q: What extinct animal came from Mars?

A: The Marstodon.

Q: How do astronauts get exercise?

A: They take moonwalks.

Q: Why would an astronaut rather go to space than to Hollywood?

A: Because there are more stars in space.

Q: Why would elephants make good astronauts?

A: Because elephants like lots of space.

Q: What's black and white and red all over?

A: A black hole sucking a candy cane.

Q: What keeps dead people from floating off the earth and into space?

A: Grave-ity.

Q: Where do astronauts buy their food?

A: At a grocery star.

Q: What are the only plants that grow on the sun?

A: Sunflowers.

Q: Why did the astronaut trip the sun?

A: She wanted to see a falling star.

Q: If the sun fell, how would it land?

A: Sunny-side up.

Q: What's the speediest thing circling the sun?

A: Fasteroids.

Q: What planet hops around the galaxy?

A: Plu-toad.

Q: Why did the astronaut take a clown to Saturn?

A: He wanted to see a three-ring circus.

Q: What would you see if the sun caught the measles?

A: Sunspots.

Q: Why will the moon never catch the measles?

A: Because it's im-moon.

Q: What planet is sleepy in the afternoon?

A: Nap-tune.

Q: What city does the sun like to go to on vacation?

A: Sun Francisco.

Q: What's the best day to go into space?

A: Fly-day.

Q: What's the best day of the week to go to Saturn?

A: Saturn-day.

Q: What day of the week is best to visit the sun?

A: Sunday.

Q: What's the best day of the week to go to the moon?

A: Moon-day.

Q: What's the scariest thing on the moon?

A: Moon-sters.

Q: What do astronauts eat on Mars?

A: The Mars-mellow.

Q: What game do astronauts play on the moon?

A: Moon-opoly.

Q: How does the sun stay clean?

A: It takes sunbaths.

Q: What does the sun put on when it goes to church?

A: Its sunbonnet.

Q: What comes out of rocket's exhaust pipes?

A: Carbon moon-oxide.

Q: Why did the astronaut want to go to Pluto?

A: Because he'd heard it was real cool.

Q: Why do astronauts borrow money from the moon?

A: Because the moon always has a few quarters.

Q: What music do astronauts like to listen to?

A: Nep-tunes.

Q: What are Nep-tunes made of?

A: Astronotes.

Q: If a boy married the sun's daughter, what would he be?

A: A sun-in-law.

Q: Where do astronauts drive their space buggies?

A: On asteroads.

Q: Who brings presents to astronauts on Christmas?

A: Sun-ta Claus.

Q: Who brings Christmas presents to Russian space travelers?

A: A Clausmonaut.

Q: When can't you visit the moon?

A: When the moon is full.

Q: What do you call three suns that all look alike?

A: A sunset.

Q: Why did the astronaut splash suntan lotion onto the sun?

A: To keep the sun from getting a sunburn.

Q: What did Jupiter say to Saturn?

A: "Why don't you give me a ring some-time?"

Q: Why did the sun try to create another planet just like Saturn?

A: Because one good Saturn deserves another.

Q: What's very, very big, very, very hot, and bites?

A: A star-antula.

Q: What would be the worst thing about living on the moon?

A: The moon-otony.

Q: When astronauts get married, where do they go?

A: On honeymoons.

Q: Where do the stars in space perform?

A: On multistage rockets.

Q: What do astronauts put on their telescopes when they want to make contact with alien creatures?

A: Contact lenses.

Q: Is the atmosphere on Jupiter fun?

A: It's a gas.

Q: Why do astronauts sometime seem conceited?

A: Because they look down on the rest of the world.

Q: How can you catch a flying saucer?

A: With a Venus flytrap.

Q: When the sun did its genealogy, what did it find?

A: Ances-stars.

Q: Who do astronauts send cards to on Mother's Day?

A: Mother Earth.

Q: How do aliens cook their food?

A: With frying saucers.

Q: Why can you trust an astronaut?

A: Because he's on the up-and-up.

Q: What was the first vegetable to orbit the Earth?

A: Spud-nik.

Q: Why do astronauts like to take-off in rockets?

A: Because it's a blast.

Q: What's the funniest thing in space?

A: Halley's Comic.

Q: Why did the astronaut dress ants in tuxedos and fly them to the moon?

A: Because he wanted to be involved with high fine-ants.

Q: What do astronauts sing to pass time while they're traveling through space?

A: "A billion bottles of Tang on the wall, a billion bottles of Tang..."

Q: If sitting too long in a chair can give you hemorrhoids, what can sitting too long in a rocket give you?

A: Asteroids.

Q: What do astronauts get if they sit on their hands all day?

A: Handroids.

Q: Where do astronauts sit when they get old?

A: In rocketing chairs.

Q: How do astronauts see in the darkness of space?

A: They use satel-lights.

Q: How do rockets communicate with each other?

A: Through intercomets.

Q: Why are astronauts rich?

A: Because they're Rocketfellers.

Q: Why did the astronaut take his dirty carpets into space?

A: Because he knew that space was a vacuum.

Q: Why did the astronaut take glass cleaner to work?

A: So he could wash the launch window.

Q: Why did the astronaut take a horse into space?

A: So he could round up the cow that jumped over the moon.

Q: Where did the cow that jumped over the moon come from?

A: The Milky Way.

Q: What did the astronaut put on his horse's back?

A: A saddle-light.

Q: What did the astronaut put his feet in?

A: The star-ups.

Q: Where do all the cows in the Milky Way come from?

A: The mooooo-n.

Q: What do a feather and the sun's rays
   have in common?

A: They're both light.

Q: What famous scientist discovered that
   our solar system has nine planets?

A: Albert Nine-stein.

Q: How did the astronaut row to the moon?

A: With an oar-bit.

Q: Why do astronauts have to go to the dentist as soon as they return to earth?

A: To get rid of the space between their teeth.

Q: Why did the astronaut put a ring through her nose?

A: Because she was a punk rocketer.

Q: Where do astronauts like to go camping?

A: In the Rockety Mountains.

Q: What basketball team do astronauts root for?

A: The Houston Rockets.

Q: What state was discovered by Martians?

A: Marssachusetts.

Q: Why did the astronaut take a walk through a clock factory?

A: Because she wanted to travel through time.

Q: What did the alien say to the first book it met on Earth?

A: "Take me to your reader!"

Q: What planet will bite you if you get too close?

A: Nip-tune.

Q: What's the quickest way to lose weight?

A: Go into space.

Q: What should you do if a baby android starts to cry?

A: Give it a robottle.

Q: What do androids sit on?

A: Their robottoms.

Q: Who are the craziest people in space?

A: The astro-nuts.

Q: Where do astro-nuts like to travel?

A: Through the loony-verse.

Q: Why did the comet scream?

A: Because the astronaut stepped on its tail.

Q: What's the difference between an alien spacecraft and a sad person with clean teeth?

A: One's a flying saucer, the other's a sighing flosser.

Q: Why is it depressing to be in zero gravity?

A: Because you feel like nothing.

Q: If a kid who can't sit still wants to be an astronaut, where should she go?

A: Into hyperspace.

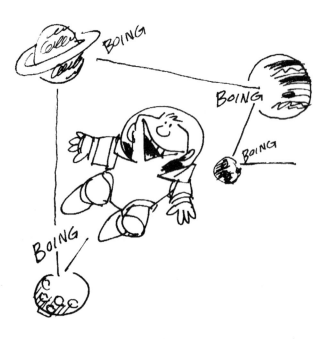

Q: Where can you find the smallest galaxies?

A: In the punyverse.

Q: If you want to blow up the moon, what do you need?

A: Am-moon-nition.

Q: If you need to tell an astronaut something while he's in space, what could you use?

A: A tell-a-scope.

Q: Why doesn't the sun own any guns?

A: Because it's not a shooting star.

Q: If the sun were a shooting star, what would it be?

A: A sun of a gun.

Q: If you're a sun of a gun, what do you need to wear?

A: A holstar.

Q: If the sun wanted a gun, what would it use?

A: One of the planets. They're all revolvers.

Q: Why does the moon hate astronauts?

A: Because astronauts can drive a moon buggy.

Q: How do we know the sun's friendly?

A: Because we can see its lights wave.

Q: Why are astronauts quiet?

A: Because NASA keeps telling them to shut-tle up.

Q: Why did the astronaut take a lamp with him in his rocket?

A: So he could travel the speed of light.

Q: What do astronauts do if they get sick in space?

A: They swallow a space capsule.